VORDS: Vinci on a roadside

Evincepub Publishing

Parijat Extension, Bilaspur, Chhattisgarh 495001

First Published by Evincepub Publishing 2018

ISBN: 978-93-88277-37-2

Price: Rs.150/-

Vinci on a roadside

By

VAZEER

ABOUT THE AUTHOR

Vazeer is a Rapper, Writer, psychologist, literary artist and a journalist. Born on 20th August 1995, comes from a simple middle class background with a mind of a visionary and a thoughtful head. Pursued his early education in NCR and later in Dehradun. He is a traveller both physically and mentally. Completed his college from Bangalore. You can find him on youtube channel bame-Hurdangg. Show some love people.

ABOUT THE BOOK

Its a collection of poetry coming out of a young observant mind. Varying from love to nation to emotion poems are words put in a manner to describe the deepest of feelings those not actually easy to say. Paper gives a mode of conversation which is not really found these days in human company.

A COLLECTION OF ENGLISH AND HINDI POEMS

CONTENT

Book 1 (English)

Book 2 (Hindi)

BOOK -1 (ENGLISH)

1- Loud Yet Silent

Dusk has fallen,
I am weak again,
Dreamy with the mountainous incarnation,
Of memories.
My eyes are foggy,
Condense with each moment passing,
Tiny droplets have kissed the edges,
Of my eyes and run down,
In steamy rills.
At this moment m nothing,
But intoxicated.
Floating on the clouds of my own past,
A journal filled with years,
As if penned down in one single night,
Repeating itself over and over again,
Night after night.
Each time a history created,
Each time history repeats itself.

VORDS: Vinci on a roadside

2 - The Invisible Man

Holding in my hand the TEDDY,
Turned THREADBARE, a gift from you,
My eyes are stuck on you,
Like a PIN in a sack.
HISTORY is present and present History,
The BRIGHT invisible man,
In his handsome COAT,
his shiny beard and thick MOUSTACHE,
Fitting into his SHOES,
A father, a true lover and life in my life.
Do i miss you?, no i don't,
Missing is for those whom we forget,
For a time.
Your still here will always be,
Etched on our soul and the air
Inside this house.
You might be gone for the world,
But i understand your trickery,
You've turned invisible,
So that you can finally see,
Our silly faces and laughable,
Moments, make silly jokes about them,
And silently laugh..
Dad, i can sense you laughing,
And i share the joke the joke with you.

3- Invitation To My World

It's an open invitation to my world,
Plzz do visit,
A place where light is still bright,
And darkness exquisite.
Come to my world,
Where work is not a necessity,
And necessity isn't work.
A place where dreams aren't burdened,
With the laws of society.
A place where decency doesn't need cover,
And shade isn't tied under the compulsion of roofs and trees.
Where clouds aren't far fetched goals,
And love still has a beautiful meaning.
So come to my world walking on silence,
Taking guidance from space,
Mixing mediocrity and distinction.
On the street of chaos and prosperity,
Amidst defiance and laws,
The last house on the lower floor,
Is Mine.

VORDS: Vinci on a roadside

4 - Illuminated Children

Illuminated children of light,
Gifted with an eye for the pernicious,
Malevolent to the malicious,
And still indifferent to society.
This where heroism turns into humanism,
A moment which turns a mere man,
Into a GOD.

5-Children of light

Children are the most illuminated,
Unlike people with burdens of society,
Neither Malevolent nor Pernicious
Blocked to the malicious world around,
And so are truly happy.
Tell me when were we really relaxed,
Or laughed like we used to years ago.
This pernicious society is stuck,
To our souls like cancer
And thus, nearly everyone is Malevolent,
Or at least selfish to a level.
Think of it, when were you last self less,
Aren't we dying inside,
No matter how well you hide it,
You're obliged to know your own truth

6 -These voices

I wish this intoxication sustains,
So i lose myself in my own tracedence,
So i praise the human mind again,
I look at the strength of it,
With crimson eyes..

I hear these voices,
From words written,
A million murmuring sounds,
I can feel the teardrop,
On the corner of the paper,
I see smiles, in these lines,
But you choked, i see you picking up the glass of water ,
You're Not here, i live you through your words..

Paradise and hell i live with you,
In these pieces of paper.

7-Scared little child

A scared little child,
Fighting for the respect of his mother,
Fighting his own family,
Denying respect to ones who don't deserve it...
And so I grew up...
I should've been a survivor,
A strong man,
But my foundations are weak,
A scared little child wishing to feel home,
And so I grew up...
Yes I had money, yes I had love,
Yes I did find what path it was,
To follow,
Yet my hands shiver when I think of the face that stays hidden,
I am terrified of my own self,
As weakness is the strength to heinous crimes,
As hate is fuel to deepest love stories.

8 -8 Am

Bright morning,
Eight Am,
Coffee and a hot balloon of thoughts,
Running through his mind.
And, so he held his pen,
Ready do pen down a fascination,
The after effect of Imagination.
And so the, the girl with umbrella,
Found a purpose again,
The dog found himself barking,
The light pose ablaze once again,
This, what is the foundation of today's reality, is,
Yesterday's imagination and
A cravat to hide the marks of labour.
We hide beneath the umbrella of clothes to be beautiful forever,
In reality every body is a book,
And every page a new 8 am,
Every chapter a new cravat,
Tighter with time, and
Every evening is a new escape.

9 -Air In your Hair

Is the goodbye, one forever?
Is life apart from the body,
You've been flowing in my soul,
Like air in your hair
Be honest, are you the almighty?

A tiny grievance from life,
How is this love so alive so soon?
Is the truth not so cozy?
Is life apart from the body,
You've been flowing in soul
Like air in your hair,
You were my love a second ago,
Oh MY, are you the almighty?

Take my hand lets move to the other side,
Let's put our faces ablaze with the light,
Never was a life like yours and mine,
Is life apart from the body?
You've been flowing in my soul
Like air in your hair,
Oh MY, are you the almighty?

10-Emotional things

Our emotions have this thing,
An obligation to be hidden,
Inside the grave they emerged in.
May a proper display gain you respect?
Does it gain you trust?
Or Does it make you close to someone?
Have you ever been out on a windy night?
The stillness of the dusk,
Accompanied with pretty much a storm.
My heart feels the same way.

Our race has this thing,
An obligation to fear for just ourselves
And so be depressed.
Its hard in this world today,
To have a true friend,
A true lover, thus, a true man.
On its run towards unknown,
Our race is forgetful,
Of us.
Thus, each person is selfish,
No one cares you're hurt,
They can pinch you harder again,
No one can decipher your tears,
If not your loneliness .
One night me hurt by word,

Sat alone into the abyss,
And thus remembered,
The law of nature.
If i was born alone,
Why am i afraid to die alone,
Am I? Yes I am.
I would think over my corpse
Of all the hearts those beat for me
In my life and the people
Who cared for me,
Yet it is utterly unbelievable,
Look at my thoughts in life.

If you think of a person over eternal peace,
Think of the only person who is happy,
In your end,
'cause the tearful will soothe and forget,
As he is forced by himself to,
But one with a smile
Will never forget..

11-Letters of Rose 1

Dear me,
Today is my last letter to myself,
I'm walking towards the lil Paradise left of me,
And my soul, to you it's Goodbye,
Don't ask me, why?
Cause this is meant of you,
'Cause this is the Sunset of the thriving Desert Rose.
Today is my last letter to myself,
'cause I'm meant to be turned
into an isolated puppet of fear.
And My Warmth, crumbled into wet sheets,
On a snowy night.

12 - Letters of Rose 2

Dear love, Remember me?
I was looking at the sunset,
It'll always be a reminder of your Goodbye.
Dear love, Remember me?
The Rose you gave died long ago,
The pages of my fav book were stained once again.
Dear love, Remember me?
Cause you leaving was a paradise lost,
Don't you dare forget me.
Serving your nation was your duty,
Trust me, I'm proud of you,
Saved a million but lost your life,
I hate you my dear love.
And now that i'm cold, It's me you save,
When did i know its you so brave,
I can feel your warmth all around me,
When each morning i hug your grave.

VORDS: Vinci on a roadside

13-Loses Tonight

Stop contemplating the loses tonight,
Look at sky, its starry bright,
I fell for you millions of years ago,
It's still Radiant, everything's alright.
So darling just hug me slow,
In this jubilant night and winter snow,
Let my breath put your heart aglow,
And let's end what we crave for.

14-Little Steve

On the hillside sat lil steve,
Year was ending, it was Christmas eve,
The streets were "jubilant" ,
But to steve's desire,
Was "craving" for "Radiant" nights,
Like the skies blazing with fire.
So he turned to the sky, to the falling star,
He could have wished for money,
But he was "contemplating" far.
He wanted a home and not just a roof,
Still a kid but in comparison aloof,
So he wished for happiness and smiles,
And not just for him but throughout the miles,
May the new year brings peace for the dying,
And brings rest for the already dead.

15 -Dead Earth

In the name of human transcendence,
We've been abusive of our soul,
Look around, all the walking dead,
Earth is the first dead planet.
Lemme tell you a story,
Story of an ugly Child,
One born hairless,
One born diff, looking diff..
His mother ran to save her child,
And succeeded, years later,
Her grandsons killed her brothers,
Destroyed their own ancestral homes,
To beautify these new ones.
Mother nature died at the hands of her own offspring.

Listen and listen close,
It wasn't us who chose this earth to live,
Instead she allowed us to propagate ,
It wasn't us who made the world a better place,
Instead this world made us a better race...

Let's ask the Gods to resurrect again,
We need him more than ever,
Cause on our own we brought this havoc,
Let's look out once again for the mother,
And let her teach us how to reign.

16 -Died just moments ago

I dreamt of it yesterday,
It happened today,
The dream interpreted death,
I died just moments ago.

My soul wanders now,
As the religion said,
I saw things proving themselves,
I saw hoaxes coming true.

One moment one wrong deed,
One right person, and life,
As a blank sheet,
One true friend, one cheat,
All it takes for history to repeat,
Itself, once again.
The best of plans and people,
The worst of outcomes,
The more peaceful you try to make this place,
The more chaotic it turns out to be,
So people once again,
Is it the upper skin?
Is it the inner beauty?
Can you see the world,
Inside your eyes?
Can you see me?

Remember I'm the wandering soul,
The base of mythology,
I am what you've been trying to discover,
Walking naked, right here with you,
Can you see the world inside your eyes?
Can you see me, deep inside?

17 -Yes he does Exist

Yes he does exist..
Your science learns compositions,
You science examines beauty,
The art of creation isn't science,
Lemme ask you the beginning of time.
It didn't start with a mere watch,
You learnt it in watches,
But you're sceptical then why,
Do you question his existence?
Well yes! He does exist.

If you were an ape,
And turned into human,
Who had turned into an ape?
Start going backwards,
let's check your limits,
'Cause trace your time no matter what,
You still just follow it,
So Mr. Human, the perfect machine,
You belong to an inventor.

So live on his might as you must,
And look at the beautiful gift you've got,
This whole world is changing just like you,
Larger with each thought,
Live and let live,
Don't be a hindrance, the mighty race,
'Cause if you question his existence,
Yes! He does exist.

18 -Yesterday Today

For what becomes yesterday,
Is right here, look close,
History is ticking away,
Behold the tides of time.

For its the mystery that sustains,
Unwrap this present slow,
Tomorrow came nearer just now,
The end is closer than you think.

Let beauty be concealed a lil longer,
Stop unveiling her face, let her eyes trench your thirst, And listen to what your heart says.

19 -Gonna fade Tomorrow

I'm not just lost anymore,
I'm completely distant to myself,
I feel, the world that surrounds me,
Is a blur.

Running away from the human transcendence,
I'm stuck inside the tunnel of what surpasses humanity,
I'm stuck between freedom and time.

Today tomorrow what matters anyway,
Its gonna fade tomorrow if not today.

20 - Wanderer of Night part 1

Wanderer of the night he was,
Walking godspeed, his lantern arched ahead.
Lit up with a bow of flames,
He could walk faster than the air..
His eyes were red, drenched with intoxication,
Of power, of fire,
Brutality had one friend, the dark.
Speaking with the air as he always liked,
Hair dangling, he gunned towards the thunder,
He had a letter to write.
Months of exclusive fire felt,
Better now..
The flames were sharper now,
like fireflies through the woods.
Running smoother now,
less devouring to the paths,
He was more human in a second,
Than a lifetime.

21-Sound of you

I hear you,
Your voice is in the air around me,
It never gets erased.
I stagger around this house,
Yelling in silence,
Trying to put up a conversation with you,
We still argue a lot,
You still make no sense.
I sleep in the same bed we used to,
Even a hundred miles away i sleep next to you,
They say youre gone for good,
I say we've never lived better.
You're yelling at me,
From the Wrinkles of these sheets,
You're right here,
I'm sitting next to you,
You're hugging me,
From the crinkles of this shirt,
You smile the same way,
I'm still falling for you,
You come and go,
In the tingling of these wind chimes,
Oh this life,so lovely,
I'm living with sound of you.

22-Archaic Soul

Different paces of time,
Distinguished in agony and aid.
I've known a lifetime in boxes,
Packs of Anger and Fear.
As if a patronage between,
Existence and Mortality.
History never omits,
No matter zest or zeal.
Childhood grows into hope,
And fades despondent.
Like sun and rain together,
Hard to fathom, yet,
So common and uncommon,
Beautiful and very unpredictable.
Memories have a hold on you,
What you were then decides,
What you are today.

My antiquity is like a Sandstorm,
Irksome, Destructive and yet,
My life which has been a desert,
With sudden oases here and there,
Remains Vital, as if an,
Archaic soul which died yesterday,
Became Nascent today.

23-Woven in my Head

WOVEN in my head is a net of thoughts,
Each thought leads to another,
And coils back to me.
Runs down a million streams my mind,
Falls Downstream from greater heights,
Louder with each thought LAID to rest,
my mind feeds me LIES,
With better Transparency each time.

24-Laid Out

This world is LAID out in a pattern. A pattern of
humane TRANSPARENCY WOVEN with LIES.
It's more and more beautiful with each step
forward, darker and darker from inside.
This world is LAID out in a web form,
WOVEN with extreme perfection.
Hanging on a thread,
running in oscillations,
With LIES on one end and TRANSPARENCY on the
other.

25-World of Misconceptions

It don't get a hang of this thing,
How people become your life ,
And one day you never see 'em back,
As they said they will,
Never get erased from your life.

Tonight fell upon a good day,
A day of laughter and smiles,
A day filled with sweet glances of friendship,
But still tonight is lonely,
But still i love the night more,
But still it's better to be frozen than molten.

In a world of misconceptions,
Love is the greatest one,
I don't mind if my skin turns blue,
I'm better numb than shivering....

26-Goosebumps

She held his hand,
His veins shivered,
She cried for him,
His heart rocked.
She touched him,
Goosebumps.
They sat and let the hearts speak..

She winked, he smiled,
She cut her hand,
Tears in his eyes,
Night and day
Day of the night,
Long desired sunlight,
Brightness all around,
And darkness became the sound of heartbeats.

His eyes are dry, her touch is gone,
His Collars are dirty,her hair blown,
His thirst,her hunger
His run, her slumber,
His heart, her life
High stakes on both sides.
His bottles on the floor
Her icecream under bed
Blood in his spit,
Her eyes turning red.

Cause dear people we all love
But the story of true love is a curse
Meant to end in tatters.

27 -Dreamt of Being a man

I dreamt of being a man,
Thought it came handy in numbers,
But i would close my eyes,
And the world went dark...
I would look at sky in a bowl of moon,
I would look at the stars,
The water moving, stars shimmering,
The moon and its scars.
I would look at sea,
Find the zenith, would try hard,
Find the soul under the sheets,
A weep beneath the bark.
I would look at the trees, heard all they spoke,
A symmetry of smiles and grief,
Under the splendid sun ,a leaf
A trash under the cars.

28 -A nation of thousand generations

A nation of thousands of generations,
A nation of generosity ,
A place which considers guests as Gods,
A place of love,
A place of reality.

A world within a boundary,
And still so free to win hearts around the world.

When i call myself an Indian,
My head is high,
My heart bowed in respect to the ones listening to me...
So raw so pure,
And yet so nasty that we scare world as one..
India, a land of struggles and peace combined,
A nation which has touched the moon and mars,
But stills bows to touch our mother's feet..
A land of respect and family ....

Proud to be an Indian.

29 - Love?

Love ?
Is it a feeling?
Or a precise evaluation.
Do you love me for myself,
Or you want me to change ?

If you ever love me,
Love me for my speech,
My words might leave you teary eyed..
If you ever love me,
Love me for my weaknesses,
Cause my strength may tear you apart.

If you ever love me
Love me for my pen,
Cause i can turn you eternal,
On a piece of paper.
If you ever love me,
Love me for my dreams,
Cause they make you my shining star.

If you ever love me
Love my fucked up self
Cause that's the true me.
If you ever love me
Love me for my lies,
Cause i'm afraid to lose you.

If you ever love me
Love me for my eyes,
Cause you'll never be homeless inside.

30 - Time is Human

It began when i understood,
That time is so human,
Obliged to change eventually.
I went down to its flowing river,
And filled a glass of moments,
Drop by drop i drank,
As if i was eternally thirsty,
And my couplet forever full.

Sip by sip my throat was sore,
As i faded in my own transcendence,
No control, No trust,
And i lost my strength.
I staggered down the aisle,
Fell upon my face,
Cried for a hand when i had two.

I stood up,
My couplet was about to dry,
Took my last sip,
And threw it behind me,
Wiped my tears with my left hand,
And clutched my right,
Tight.
I wasn't staggering anymore..

What i don't remember is,
When did this lake emerged inside me,
I can feel the longing for a stone,
To stir the stillness of this lake,
To unreachable corners ..

31 - Bleed Quitely

I don't know what these words mean,
If m trying to express or hide deeper,
If bleed quietly or,
Rundown by patches of crimson.

My head throbs with desires,
Of being someone I know,
I look at the mirror and wonder,
Why is this face pale as snow?
Look at my thoughts,
They wander a million streets,
As if i am the wind,
With no house no land,
Still under the sheets.

Am i lost or hidden by choice,
Can you see me,
Or you just blindfolded?
Are you guilty or I am,
Is this pain or shame ?

32 - I wander

This, what is tormented hurts
and the light is dead,
i wander.

Last night i was startled by the voice of a silhouette, and
i yelled who are you?
He said, wandering.

There used to be a lil world,
Right inside this head,
The world has frozen in silence.
I wander.

I realised my fear,
It actually came from emptiness,
'Cause loneliness pats you down.
I wander.

33-Sons of a Nation

A scared mother,
A shivering daughter,
A numb wife,
A proud father..
Who left forever were sons,
Sons of a nation.

Mom: The standing tall who smiled at me , last i saw him, Is this tattered body the same one? My son? Is this the same child i fed? My son? People speaking around the tales of martyrdom, Tales of whom? This tattered body , Or my son?

Dad: The one who used to fear my scolds, People say he died fighting some cranky killers. Is this true? I say am proud , VERY PROUD, but my eyes are watery, my cheeks are wet, my wife is nearly unconscious, but this person dead of holes, is my son. Is this true?

*Daughter: *SILENCE* Is the nation mistaken again. They say he is my father , but i can't see the same hands which used to hug me. Where is that smiling face who would come to me and lift me up off my feet and put me close to his chest and say you my girl are the pride of my life.*

Wife: The one i saw my life with, the one i saw my hopes in, the one i loved with my whole heart, never beared a single scratch on him. I ask you , Is this a real duty? IS this a real fate?

34-What is reality?

Reality is what, if not silence,
a close mouthed intent to say ,
and listen to the silence.
Reality is what, if not a mind full of sounds loud as hell,
if not an adrenaline rush,
for the thought of reality.
Reality is nothing that goes on and off just sit and think
what is reality,
what you heard?
what you said?
what you thought?
what you perceived?
Or reality is only thing in this world that you don't
know.

I ask what is the truth?
what is happening or what should've happened ?

35 -Night of Horror ascends

I'm not sure of anything anymore,
I'm picking up the broken pieces of my psyche,
As the time to my great horror ascends,
I dig deeper in my melancholy soul,
Sour, with pain and immese hurting.

It beats slower now,
Drops of vain, minted in the flow
And my veins hurt,
With every move,
And so it bent me down,
Laid me to rest,
The world i assumed,
To be clutched in my hands,
Scattered like sand,
On the tides of time.

Sometimes i think how would i,
Sit through the night of my horror,
With an aching psyche,
As if a broken mirror,
I wish to go deeper,
Find the broken pieces,
But one lost in eternity
Is difficult to retrieve.

They talk about things,
Which doesn't kill us,
Makes us stronger.
So nothing makes us weak?
So nothing pains this heart?
No words cut that deep?
Yes,they do, don't they?

Sometimes somethings,
Some words or even blinks,
Can come so close to heart
That is really hard to forget,
Not yesterday, Not today,
Not Tomorrow.

36-Before I fall

The red dawn, the inner sky,
eminent bright,
fall of the flight of dark,
into the meadows of sun,
Winning again with a heavy heart,
making it sink deeper,
And the art of glory.
The difficult smile trying,
to take over the edge of the eyes,
and swelling upon,
The emotions waivered,
and blinks stuck in lashes,
everytime a pain of psyche,
and mended by the,
heavy beating of heart.
Tonight the confusion of each word,
derived from air of hurtfulness
And the shadows of the dark
appear in front of the light
turning a dusk all around,
from up to down.
Each word left unsaid,
Each emotion killing,
Dead, Gone, Dried.
AND HERE I STAND,
A MOMENT BEFORE I FALL.

37 -Strands of Time

Strands of time where may paas,
logics and sarcasm,
barefoot, and rip you off your clothes,
and then shed blood each drop,
drain...
the bowl of birth, the cloudy heaven,
the only reason to detain,
and feel the way only towards
down or up
meant or not, have to abate
or terminate.
This is the face of earth,
the foundation of socialism,
the founder of cannibals..
and may give a reason for humans to grow,a reason
to fall and stand up stroger,
or vanish in the face of soil...
AS I MAY STAND TONIGHT,
ON URGE OF MY OMISSION

38 - I am the soul of Earth

I am the soul of earth
I am the voice of rain
together with the wind blows
shivering cries and crying pain.
the depth of heart
the immense of hurt,
twice the face covered,
the tweaked shirt.
the shivering sense of blood,
the quivering sense of vain,
together with the wind blows,
shivering cries and crying pain.

39 -Endure

I could hold my breath
and endure
feel hard and never utter a word
can take slaps right in my face
and wont wish for shoulders I could lean on,
in the race.
I would say no matter,
if i'm alone,
no matter, if my legs hurt,
I would run faster with each breath,
and hit the goal right in the centre of it.
I would fake it,
till I make it,
would hide it,
till I speak it.
I am made of skin and
bones hard enough to break a wall,
of words hard enough to imitate silence,
and thoughts hard enough to crack a skull.

40 -This is Rage

I'll love you the most in this world so that your guilt kills you and tears you apart into two halves so when each time you look at me you kill yourself inside just to keep yourself quite. I'll make sure that everything I do is for you too so that whenever you look at yourself you see me in ur other half and then try to close your eyes to stop the guilt from turning them crimson like blood. You'll face a death every time I am in front of you, everytime I touch you, hold you, smile at you or even just give you a dry glance. I'll love you so much that your guilt will turn into shame and you'll try to run away from it yet you can't because even if you leave me far behind my love will stalk you in your mind. But still the last card has to be thrown that when you leave i'll cry to the fullest till I drain myself out, of all the tears and fears and miseries, this taste of blood will leave my mouth too. The day when someone accepts you like I did you wont be able to face the reality that you are a cheat and a betrayer ,slayer of a heart that cried your name on its each beat and you'll find me again in your breath. I'll be there on the day when you ask "can I kill myself?" and my answer will be no cause yet more pain has to be suffered so you won't die until you see my corpse burnt into ashes, until the heat of those flames remind you of my hugs, until the beating of those flames against ur face reminds you of my kisses, you'll never be free of me even in your death you'll die a million times,you couldn't value my love so this time this is RAGE.

BOOK -2 (HINDI)

41-Bass chala jaa raha

Kuch baato ko aaj seene me rakhe,
Bass chala jaa raha, bass chala jaa raha.
Kuch khwahisho ko aakho me rakhe
Bass chala jaa raha bass chala jaa raha.

Kuch ranjishein, kuch bandishein
Kuch raahtein, kuch chahatein
Kuch dooriyan, majbooriyan
Kuch hasratein, kuch mannatein
In kaato pe yun aakho ko moonde,
Bass chala jaa raha, Bass chala jaa raha.

Beetabiyan, bechainiyan
Nazdikiyan, ye yaariyan,
Yu hoke ye dhoke
Hume daste rahein, dil me baste rahein
Yun hoke log saare,
Humpe haste rahein, taane kaste rahein,
Yaado ke dhue se bani,
Ye vaadiyan, ye ghaatiyan
In sab ko aaj hotho pe rakhe,
Bass chala jaa raha, bass chala jaa raha.

42 -Akhri Makan

Kabhi aana mere mohalle,
To ana gali ke kone tak,
Kone ki imarat ka nichla makan mera hai,
Inn chand diwaro ko,
Mai ghar bolta hu.
Kholna dhyan se uss darwaze ko,
Ek maa ki riwayatein basti hain,
Kayi muskurahtein tairati hain,
Uss ghar ki hawao me,
Kayi aansuo ke daag, mite nahi ab tak.
Kabhi darwaze ke iss paar aao,
To dhyan se sunna sannate ko,
Sannata jisme ek baap ki,
nasihatein goonjti hain.
Mere ghar ki khushboo me sahej ke saans lena,
Har dam par maa ke hoth mehsoos honge,
Maathe par,
Har saans, mere baap ke haath,
Peeth thap thapa denge tumhari.

Aankhe mat moondna,
Bade sundar khwab dikhte hain,
Inn pardo ke saaye me,
Dilkash lamhe muft me bikte hain,
Kone ki imarat ka nichla makan,
Mera hai,
Kabhi aana mohalle, to ana gali ke kone tak.

43 - Akhand Bharat Hu.

Mai suryami aakash ka ugta suraj,
chamchamata chand hu,
Mai achal amar shram ka vishram hu
Shaan se mai jal raha
Lahu luhan chal raha,
Na thakta hu na ghat ta hu,
Na chat ta hu, na bat ta hu,
Mai shambhu ka trishul,
Rasul ke jeevan ki dhul,
Mai karm ka kaarath hu,
Mai hi hu, mai akhand bharat hu
Aaj khand khand pal raha hu,
Saam daam chhal raha hu,
Anamika ka maan me,
Soch se vifal hua hu,
Mai taam hu, rajas bhi hu,
Atharva hu, ayur bhi hu,
Raam ka main naam hu,
Khuda ke dar ki shaan hu,
Mai bhor ka prakash hu,
Shaam ka mai jaam hu,
Arjun ka indraprastha hua,
Kabhi mai aryavart hua,
Mai aaj bhi khada hu dekh,
Jhuk ke bhi samasth hua,
Kabhi dev, kabhi shyam
Dagmagate rath ka saarath hu,
Mai hi hu, akhand bharat hu.

44-Ghar me Maa aayi hai

Dhul rahi hai chamache katoria din me teen teen dafe,
Aaj thalio se apnepan ki khusboo fir ek baar aayi hai,
Yun to jeevan chal raha tha apni raaftar me, aur bhi din,
Par aaj bade dino baad, ghar me Maa aayi hai.
Paani se bharne ko gilase taras gayi thi,
Kuch bartan dukhi pade the kono me,
Chadrei jinko pucha nahi kafi dino se kisi ne,
Aaj unke chehre pe bhi muskaan aayi hai,
Aaj bade dino baad, ghar me Maa aayi hai. Yu to khirkiya khadkhadati nahi,
Darwaze ki chokhat se padosan paar aati nahi,
Maine dekha nahi par yakeen hai ki aaj
Balcony me kursiya chaar aayi hai,
Aaj kayi dino baad, ghar me Maa aayi hai.
Ghar ke kone kone bhi jee uthe hain firse,
Parde bhi laher maarte hain,
T.V. bhi menu card leke taiyaar khada hai,
Aur kadhayi aaj phir Istemal Aayi hai,
Aaj kayi dino baad ghar me, maa aayi hai.
Chup baitha rehta tha mai iss kamre mai,
Kayi dino se phone ki call log badhti ja rhi thi,
Raat bhar andhera rehta hi tha,
Par jaane kyun neend nahi aa rahi thi,

Sooni padi diwaro me aaj jaise bahar aayi hai,
Kyuki aaj bade dino baad, ghar me Maa aayi hai.
Ab subah shaam har din chai bhi banegi,
Aur ghr aane me deri par phone ki ghanti bhi bajegi,
Ab school jaane ki taiyari bhi roz hogi,
Kabhi kabhi ghamasan bahes bhi chidegi,
Kabhi zarurat pe jhaadu lagegi,
To kabhi bina wajah pocha,
Kal ke pehne kapde bhi dhul jayenge,
Aur awaz ye bhi ayegi beta sab band kr aur khana kha,
Aaj zindagi me zindagi phir ik baar aayi hai,
Kyon Ki bade dino ke baad, ghar me Maa aayi hai.

VORDS: Vinci on a roadside

45 -Anjaan Firse Ho Gaya

Apne dhundta dhundta mai, yaha se waha gaya,
Desh choda apna to, anjaan firse ho gaya,
Yahi hai sachai meri,
Jisko paya kho gaya,
Chamakta hua mai chand tha,
Toota tara ho gaya...
In anjaan rasto pe,
Mai awara ho gaya,
Kabhi jo hass na paya to,
Mai beechara ro gaya..
Aaj ki ye baat nahi,
Kafi arsa ho gaya,
Dilo ko jeet ta hua,
Mai khud hi khud ko kho gaya...
Mai kal ki socha karta tha,
Ab mai kal ka socha karta hu,
Mai bekhauf chalta tha,
Ab har kadam sambhalta hu,.
Mai raat me prabal hua,
Andher me achal hua,
Tu chod de mujhe yahi,
Jaha ke kal beeta tha,
Jaha ke kal bhi ho gaya.

46- Ye Dastaan-e-Gumaan

Shidatt ki is siyahi se likhi,
Ye dastan-e-gumaan,
Ho behki si meri, jo mehki si teri,
Ho aankhon ki ye putliyan.

Mai hu pathik ban ja meri ghata si,
Chal chaat dein milke ab ye udaasi,
Le haath thaam banja meri tu saathi,
Aur todd de ab ye meri bebaaqi.

Jo tu muskura toh teri raahon mein,
Yun palke bichaye se hum let jaayein,
Jo sharma de tu to, teri haya me,
Ek rangeeli muskaan, hum phet jaayein,
Aa nazrein milayein, aa parde girayein,
Aa krne lagein hum bhi gustakhiyan,
Jo halki si meri, jo chalki si teri,
Ho aankhon ki ye putliyan.

47 -Khuda Bhi

khuda bhi aasma se jab zameen pe dekhta hoga,
tu kitni khoobsoorat hai, ye khud se puchta hoga.
tere jism se jhadte ho jaise paak kamal,
teri boli azan ki aahat lagti hai,
jispe jhukte hai sir khuda ke darbar me,
teri chuvan ja namaz lagti hai.
teri aakho me dekh kar allah bhi,
teri rooh pe naaz karta hoga...
tu kitni khoobsoorat hai ye khud se puchta hoga.
imambade ki chaukhat ka sharaf mile,
jo tere labo se kisi ke lab mile,
asgar ko pani ki aas na ho,
jo akhri waqt me tujhse nazar mile,
tu jannat ka darwaza ho jaise,
tujhe paale koi to zindagi ka maqsad mile.
tere nakshe nazm ko jibraeel,
sone se likh ke rakhta hoga...
tu kitni khoobsurat hai wo khud se puchta hoga..
khuda bhi asma se jab zameen pe dekhta hoga,
tu kitni khoobsurat hai wo khud se puchta hoga.

48-Abhi isi pehlu

Mujhe dekhne de abhi isi pehlu,
Meri nazar ko tujhse guzarne ki zaroorat hai,
Aarzoo khuli aakho se behter lagti hai,
Aur kabhi ye bhi lagta hai ki,
Aage badh kar chu liya usko...
Aur tammna zara bhar aur mukkamal ho gyi..

Yahi hai zindagi, yahi hum dono hai,
Tum aarzoo aur mai uska ehsaas,
Tum ek khoobsurat sapna ho
Aur mai subah ko dimag me ataki
Wo dhundli tasveer, hum dono ka wajood
Ek dusre ke bina adhoora hai.

49 - Shaitaan Badal hi Jata hai

Jeevan ki law par to dekho Insan pighal hi jaata hai,
Tum Ayina gar Dedo to shaitaan Badal hi Jata hai,
Badal hai ye ik Paani ka Jo phat kr bhi garjayega,
Paani fir Lekin Paani hai, kuch daag Mita kr Jata hai.
Chal hum bhi fir takrayenge yaado ke teekhe mod par ,
Kuch hum bhi teer chala lenge beete panno Ko khol kar ,
Jin panno Ko padhna me ab bhi, tanha Dil ghabrata hai,
Kuch kehna Sunna hi to hai jo gaatho Ko suljhata hai,
Tum Ayina gar Dedo to shaitaan Badal hi jata hai..
Iss dakiyanoosi dunia ke sab dharre nakare hain,
In dharro par jo haar Gaye wo sab Pyaare bechaare hain,
Zanjeero me aage badh kr jo sir ucha chillata hai,
Bass ek Wahi hai jo Jag me mar kar zinda reh Jata hai ,
Tum Ayina gar dedo to shaitaan Badal hi Jata hai..
Ye waqt ki aisi Seema hai sab chehre palte jaate hain ,
Jab jebein Khali Hoti sab saaf Nazar me aate Hain,
Ye Hasna Rona Jeevan ka Lamba pehlu le Jata hai,
Tum ayina gar Dedo to shaitaan Badal hi Jata hai.

50 - Kabhi

Kabhi kisi se mann hi mann sawal kiya hai, Ke kyu ab unki awaz bhi sunai nahi deti?
Kabhi socha hai ki kal tum yahi the?
To ab kaha ho ke jab tumhari zaroorat hai?
Kabhi yaad kiya hai guzra zamana?,
Agar ha to tum wahi ho jaha mai hu...

Kabhi akelepan ka sahara khoya hai?
Kabhi dard me marham na mila ho?
Kabhi yuhi tapte tadapte raat bitayi hai?
Ya uss raat me arsa beet gaya ho?
Agar ha to tum wahi ho jaha mai hu....

Tum bhi to yahi the, the na,
Kuch nahi to ek aas thi,
Aaj kyun talash ki surat uthaye mai tanha hu fir?
Kabhi socha hai ki wo kaha hoga?
Inn bujhti mashalo se firr jal gayi ungli,
Aur andhere me saaye bhi saath chodd gaye,
Kabhi khud se khud ka rasta dhunda hai?
Kabhi socha hai manzil pe tanha hona kya hoga?

VORDS: Vinci on a roadside

51-Huqumat Karne walo

Kabhi kabhi jee karta hai,
badal lu apne bhes ko,
Niklu sadko par chillane,
ke badlo mere desh ko,
Kabhi nirbhaya, kabhi asifa
ye kya bawal kr dala hai,
Huqumat karne walo, desh ka kya haal kar dala hai...
Patthar ke tan pe sona hai,
Par sabke ghar me rona hai ,
Sawal karo to kehte hai,
Jo hona hai so hona hai,
Maaye darti andhero se ,
Bahene darti savero se ,
Bhai, baap gar chinn jaye,
ghar bhuka marne wala hai,
Huqumat karne walo, desh ka kya haal kar dala hai.
Wo bhi kya ek zamana tha,
jab desh par shaan hum karte the,
imaan pe jaan bhi dete the ,
Pardon me jannat hoti thi,
Aur chain ki saansein bharte the ,
Unn khushnuma yaado ko tumne
behaal kr dala hai ,
huqumat karne walo, desh ka kya haal kr dala hai

Seema pe rozz ladai hai ,
swiss bank me rakhi kamai hai ,
Mehnat krne wale ke ghr me
Sasti sabzi aayi hai,
Bharat ki pak zameen ka jaise,
Vahishkaar kar dala hai ,
Huqumat karne walo desh, ka kya haal kar dala hai. ...
Baapu ke khwaab bhi toot gaye,
Iss desh ke apne rooth gaye,
Haram ki khane wale sab,
Halal ka swad hi bhool gaye,
Chacha ke nanhe bacho ko,
Patthar dil hi kar dala hai,
Huqumat karne walo desh ka kya haal kar dala hai
.

52 - Heera

Khayalo ki udantashtari se latka wo heera,
Kanch ki tarah bikhar raha hai hawaon ke manch par.
Tamasho se ke kat kr, tarash raha hai shor me,
Laraz ki talash me baarish khojta hai.
Kaifiyat-e-khayal iska angushtari ki shaan hona nhi hai,
Kisi gudaaz gale ka armaan hona nhi h,
Ye mehrum-e-zamana ataka hai un andher khadano me ,
Ke jaha ye lakho ka ek nahi, lakho me ek tha.
Iss Insani tarannum ne ise kya bana dala hai,
Gumaan bhi krte hain to keemat laga kr.
Jisse zewar banate hain wo zaherila hai duniya bhar se mazboot ,
Ye jung-e-shaan hai ya maidan-e-jung,
Sajawat hai ya taiyaari fateh ki?
Ye gale lagane nikle hain ya lahoo bahane nikle hain?

53-Aayina

Mai bas ek mai janta hu,
Ki tu kaun hai.
Maine tera haal dekha hai,
Bezaar dekha hai, behaal dekha hai,
Maine teri kashish dekhi hai,
Tujhe kamal dekha hai.
Mai chup hu awaz ka maara hu,
Mai bol raha hu in chatakte kono se,
Tujhe badalna chah raha hu.

Ek mai, bass mai dekh sakta hu
Teri muskaan ka asli mayina ,
Tubhi kabhi mujhme jhaak kar dekh,
Aye Meri mohabbat mai tera ayina.
Jab kabhi tere chehre pe gam hota hai,
Teri aakho ke zariye mera dil bhi nam hota hai,
Chal aa iss athaah gehrai me dubte hain meri jaan,
Aye meri mohbatt dekh idhar, mai tera ayina...

Tera bachpan mehfooz rakha hai maine,
Teri khushi, tera rang bhi,
Teri chahat, tera gam bhi ,
Aur mai tujhe dusro ki bahon me sambhalta hu,
Jab tu usme doob jaati hai, tera aashiqui wala
chehra nikalta hu,
Kabhi asliyat dikhai jab, tu mujhse dur ho gayi,

VORDS: Vinci on a roadside

Kabhi mujhse takrayi tu, teri yaadein chur ho gayi,
Tut kar bhi mai tujhe apne saath leke jata hu,
Ek naye andaaz me fir wapas milne aata hu,
Mai teri ankho ki sujan ka rehbara
Aye meri mohabbat sun mai mai tera ayina.

54-Alag hu, Akela hu

Mai alag hu, isliye akela hu....
Zamane se yaari karke dekhi hai,
Dushmani bhi nibhayi hai,
Ghr bhi chodd ke dekha hai,
Maa ki yaad bhi aayi hai...
Kaha jau ki mai mai rahu,
Mai yaari, dosti, pyar, mohabbat,
Har naksh ko jhela hu,
Mai alag hu, isliye akela hu.

Tu chale na sang mere to fark nahi padta,
Ye mai kehta hu mera dil nahi kehta,
Mai wahi rehta hu kiran ke kone pe,
Wo jo drishti ka aakhri chor hai, haan wahi,
Haatho pe haath rakh vaade ab nahi hote,
Tu mere saath hai par mai wahi pe baitha hu,
Mai alag hu,shayad isiliye akela hu.

55 -Bikhre Rishte

Wo rishte bikhre pade hain Zameen par,
Kuch karchein pairo me aksar chubh jaati hain,
Baat ajeeb hai ki mai baith jata hu,
Aur ye aankhen nami se jhuk jati hain.

Un rishto ki khushboo bass gayi hai jati nahi,
Jane kya bolu, koi baat samajh aati nahi,
Tere faisley se samjhota kar mai aa gaya is taraf,
Kambakht meri rooh hai ki iss paar aati nahi.

Tere haathon ke nishaan hai meri jild par,
Mitane me lagta hai, chehra badal jayega,
Bair haal umeed ka patthar akta hai gale me,
Garmi badhegi ek din, patthar pighal jayega...

Tera naam lene me zubaan ladkhadane lagi hai,
Sab chehro ki rangat saaf nazar aane lagi hai,
Pherti hogi muh duniya jaan ke asliyat,
yaha to zidd bhi aur zidd khane lagi hai...

Chaand ki roshni andhere roshan krti hai,
andhere mita nahi paati,
har amavasya pe ek chand mar jata hai,
uski maut pe roshni nazar nahi aati..

Koodte honge log dariya me kinaro ki khatir,

hume to lehron ke saath hi jeena qubool hai,
kinaro pe baitha thak chuka hu mai,
jaise zindagi ka har pal ek katra dhool hai.

Jaane kiss bhool ki maafi nahi hoti,
saza-e-maut bhi ek tarike se muafi hai,
Halaq khushk hai cheekh cheekh kar mera, Shayad
zindagi me chup hona hi baaki hai.

56-Zaroori thi, Zaroori hai

Mai koshish karta hu
ki kuch aisa likhu, teri aakhe nam ho jayein,
par mujhe kewal teri muskaan yaad hai,
kya likhu ki tu muskura de.
Matha teku to shayad mannat puri ho,
nazar uthau aur tujhe dekh lu.

Bhari sadak, har chehre par meri aakhein hain,
hotho pe chand lamhe hain,
dil me athaah yaadein hain,
mujhe pehle lamhe bhi mohabbat thi tujhse,
meri aaj bhi tujhpe jaan jaati hai...
kuch naksh tere chehre se milte ho jiske,
wo surat hume yun hi pasand aa jati hai...

Mere qatil meri duniya me ek pal,
tum jo aaye the,
ke jaane kyun ye lagta hai,
ki fursat tum hi laye the,
zamano se ye dharti jal rahi hai,
aag deti hai,
Kabhi mehsoos hota hai,
ki baarish tum hi laye the...

Ye manzil betuki si hai,
adhuri thi adhuri hai,
tere aashiq ko jaana tu,
zaroori thi, zaroori hai.

57-Fir yaad aa rahi hai

Aaj fir kisi yaad si aa rahi hai,
Aaj fir ek arzoo paida ho gayi,
Har baar ki tarah ghanti rukne se pehle,
Mann hi mann baatein taiyaar hongi meri,
Har baar ki tarah ye baat cheet bhi,
Isi ghanti pe khatam ho jayegi....,
Dheere dheere saaf hua,
Ashiqui ki rangat badal gayi,
Naraz hu mai aaj phir aashiqui se,
Aashiq ke seene pe phir churi chal gayi..

Dekh kar andekha kiya tha unhone,
Wo akhri mulakat aaj bhi yaad hai,
Chaand us raat bhi adhura tha,
Aur aaj bhi andheri raat hai...
Baat choti si sahi,
Magar baat bahut saaf hai,
Aashiq ko deewangi ka saath,
Bada kharab hai...

Lut rahe hain moti aaj phir
anginat taadat me,
Sab ke chehro pe aaj ashiqui ki zeenat hai,
toote tukdo pe roshni chamakti hai,
par,
Timir ke saagar me inki kya keemat hai,

Kheech kr chaadrein andher ki patak to zameen par,
Phir dekho,
Aankhen jalti hain duniya ki dhoop me,
Yeh kaid hai jannat ke roop me,
Main ghut raha hu apne andar dheere dheere,
Aur tera khud se bhaagna mustaid h, chahat ke roop me.

58-Tujhi se door ho gaye

Chahat thi iss qadar teri,
Ki ishq-e-magroor ho gaye,
Tere itne hue qareeb jana,
Ki aaj tujhi se door ho gaye.

Teri aahatein Oojhal hui,
Hum pal pal majboor ho gaye,
Tere itne hue qareeb jana
Ki aaj tujhi se dur ho gaye.

Bante rahe tamasha hum,
Teri muskaan ki khatir,
Girte rahe uthte rahe,
Tere aakho ke jaam ki khatir,
Teri in abaad galiyon me,
Hum be-abroo se mashoor ho gaye,
Tere itne hue qareeb jana,
Ki aaj tujhi se dur ho gaye.

VORDS: Vinci on a roadside

59-Ankho ke dar.(re-written)

Main aakho ke dar milu na agar
Toh chehra mera ye awaz hai,
Jo dhunde kabhi tu, mujhe dar badar
Mera aaina ye awaz hai...

Ho andhera kabhi ho raatein ghani,
Ho madham larazti si woh chandni,
Toh tu muskura kar, yun nazre chura kr,
Apni palkon ki chadar tale dekhna,
Kuch roshan se khwabo ka jalta dia,
Tere kaano mein padti ye awaz hai,
ye awaz hai.

Kabhi yun bhi ho ke sahil pe tu,
Samandar ki lehro taraf dekh kar,
Thakti ungli, jaane kyu saw martaba,
Likhe, geeli ret pe naam mera,
Jo lehre mitayengi uss naam ko,
Woh sang me layi ye awaz hain.
Ye awaz hai.

Mai aakho ke dar milu na agar
Toh chehra mera ye awaz hai...

60-Zindagi takaze deti rahi

Zindagi har din takaze deti rahi,
Isi andaaz se andaze deti rahi,
Choti si jheel me samandar sama gaya,
Aansu ki aankh mein tamashe deti rahi...

Shabdo ke kafno tale dabe beeti hai,
Andhere ki aad me sapne piroti hai,
Iss zindagi ka jaane khel hi ajab hai,
Zuban ke teer dil ko chubhoti hai...

Aankho ke raste zahen kharoch diya,
Zakham dekar marham bhi de diya,
Nafrat aati hai aisi zindagi pe,
Sab kuch de diya, Sab kuch le liya....

Khwab khwab hai adhure reh jate hain,
Zindagi ke raste poore kaha jaate hain,
Toot jata hai rahgir kahi beech raste mein,
Zakham adhoore bhi ho daag poore reh jate hain..

VORDS: Vinci on a roadside

61 -Yado ke dariya me

Talafuz chadta jata hai, alfaaz utarte hain,
Hum apki yaado ke dariya mein, har raat utartein hain,
Yeh shabdo ki neev hai mahengi hai, mazboot bhi,
Yahin tumse kayam hain hum, yahin majboor bhi.
Nasha chadta jata hai, Sawalaat utarte hain,
Bheegi palko se dilo ke halat utarte hain.

Na iltija-e-tasleem rahi, na bairhan deedar hua,
Mere hi dil ka tukda, mere dil ke paar hua,
Chalte hain pair iss khurd rah par mere,
Par teri galiyo se hum bezaar guzarte hain.
Hum teri yaadon ke dariya mein, har raat utartein hain.

Jo kabhi apna na tha, usse khone ka kaisa gham,
baat adhuri hi thi ki, baat khatam,
hoto pe hasi hai, dil mein angaar utarte hain,
hum teri yaadon ke dariya me har raat utartein hain.

62-kuch chittiyan rakhi hain teri

Kuch chittiyan rakhi hai teri,
Aaj bhi mere sandook me.
Kuch safey hamara qissa bayan karte hain.
Dekhta hu teri likhai ko,
Toh teri awaz sunai deti hai,
Nazrein hata lu gar panno se,
Toh tu dikhai deti hai...
Kuch nahi ek raat thi,
Saher par ojhal ho gayi,
kuch nahi ek bikhri kahani thi,
palko pe bojhal ho gayi...
Tujhe bhi paya tha,
maine naseebo se,
Tujhe bhi kho baitha,
Kuch khote sikko sa,
Jantri ka panna palta,
Jannat palat gayi,
Tehkhana saja hai mere,
khwabon ke naseebo sa...
Kabhi kabhi sochta hu kaash,
Main bhi dikhta mere raqeebo sa,
Hota wahi kahin aas paas
Rehta tere habibo sa...

63-Dar par Tere

Ek patthar rukh aya tha dar par tere,
Jis din se tune mujhe chod diya,
Aaj palta gaya, tere dar par,
Aur wo patthar bhi phod diya...
Jin rahon se katrata tha,
Un raho se muh mod liya,
Mai bhitar bhitar marta hu,
Tujh par marna bhi chod diya.

Ek raat kati andhere mein,
Andhere baad bhi andhera tha,
Wo khwab mujhe jagaye hai,
Jo khwab kisi din mera tha.
Kya rasta tha kya manzil thi,
kya raat thi kya savera tha,
Thehra tha logo ki bheed mein,
Sehra pe mai akela tha..

64-Tumhe mai naa dhundu bhale

Tumhe mai chand sitaro mein na dhundu bhale,
Mai tumko kayi tehkhano mein dhundunga..
Meri yaado ke jaalo me lipta ke rakhunga tumhe,
kitabo ke panno pe chaap k rakhunga....
Tum mere asli rang ka akhri nishan ho,
tumhare piche ke sab mita chuka tha mai,
Ab ye rangat aakho me utar hi aayi hai,
Toh tumhe khwabo me basa ke rakhunga..
Tu dur bhi rahe to mere dil me hai,
karib se chuye to rooh chu leti hai,
jab zarra zarra tere naam se roshan hu,
to tujhe dil andhero me basa ke rakhunga..
Saari ranjishe tujhse, saare hal bhi tu,
tu meri tamanna mai teri aarzoo,
jab tammna adhuri, aarzo bhi adhuri hai,
to tujhe aankho ki nami me saja ke rakhunga...

65-Halat-e-Iltija

Halat-e-iltija thi ki tasleem ho,
Humne tumhari or kya dekh lia,
Nazare tham gayi.
Kuch bade sawal yaad aaye,
kuch chote lamhe,
Waqt ik dafe fir piche ho gya.

Mai janta hu tumhari aankho ka rang kya hai,
Uss rangat ke nishaan aaj bhi hai seene par mere.
Jo kuch lamhe mai utha laya tha tumhari chaukhat se,
Aaj bhi meri baaton mein shamil hain.

Tera naam lene se rokta hu khud ko,
Sunne se dur bhagta hu,
Woh har cheez jo teri yaadon ke bojh uthaye hai,
Kandho se utaar chuka hu kabka,
Par ba khuda ye zubaan tere naam par aaj bhi,
Ladkhada jati hai.

Wo chand lamhe jo tham gaye tumhe dekh ke,
Mere ye khayal the un lamho me,
Tumhara kehna raha ki maine bolna chod diya,
Meri aas rahi ki kaash tum sun paati.

66-Gehraiyaan

Ek din maine khayalo ka ek reza liya,
Rezey ko gooth ke dor kardi,
Aur dor khichta hua mai,
Le gaya falak tak...

Falak ke darwaze par udd rahe badal
Jaise udano ko pehredaari krte ho,
Mujhse takra gaye.
Manzil me rukawat dekh,
Khayalo me hakarat aa gyi
Aur hum bhi badalo se rajinsh kr baithe,
Kuch yun,
Ki falak roshan ho utha,
Barisho ne khayalo me,
Nadiya baha di,
Maano baghbani puri ho gyi..

Ruaab me utar kr sahil par,
Maine nadi ko gahraiyo ko takaza de diya,
To nadi boli
Ki aao tum bhi hamare sang tairo,
Doob ke dekho samandaro mein
Ki gahrayio ke maniye kya hote hain.

67 -Papa

Papa ko meetha buhut pasand hai,
Aur shayad acting bhi...
Isiliye to smjh nahi aata ki kab dukhi hai,
Aur kab bhout zyada khush.
Maine aaj tak papa ke muh se
Pareshan hu nahi suna,
Aur ye bhi nahi ki mai aur logo jaisa kyu nahi hu.
Pata hai, papa apni zindagi me qaid hai,
Taaki mai azad reh saku,
Taaki mai udd saku,
Aur shayad wo paa saku wo unhone qurbaan kar diya,
Sukoon.
Mere liye saal me chaar baar shopping karne wale,
Mere papa, apne liye chaar saal me ek baar kuch lete nazar aate hain.
Jo cheez pasand bhi aati hai use
kuch khaas nahi keh ke chod dete hai..
Sach kahu to hum sab thode laalchi hai,
Par papa apni salary ka ek ek paisa humpe khrch dete hain.
Wo mere papa hi hai jo apni mehnat se
Mere liye aram kamate hai,
Apni mehnat ki kamayi ko,
Mujh Par udate hain.
Har din rozz taiyaar hokar ek hi kaam krte hue

thakte nahi,
Par aksar hi mauka milte hi so jaate hain.
Papa boring nahi hai, bass mann ki baatein bol nahi paate,
Aur hum hain ki ankahi baatein sunn nahi paate.
Mere papa mere hero ho na ho,
Par wo meri pehchan ka sabse pehla hissa hai,
Aur mujhe apni pehchan pe garv hai.

68 -Teri purani chittiyan

Aajkal, teri or dekhta hu,
Toh teri purani chittiyan yaad aati hai.
Teri awaz ki kasak aati hai unse.
Jin baato pe zubaan tham jaati hai ab,
Unn baato ka raks aaj bhi labo pe mehsoos hota hai?
Kisi zamane mein, ek zamana tha,
Ki jab lagta tha, tere labb meethe hain,
Kambakht ye khiza kuch yu beeti,
Ki ab tere bol chubh jaate hain...
Yaad hai kaise raat kahanio ke tale bitai thi,
Yun lagta tha tu mere bagal me leti hai,
Main teri zulfo se khel raha hu,
Tu meri aankho me jaakh rahi hai....
Kahani shayad wo nahi thi jo tune suni, maine kahi,
Kahani wo raat thi, jo beet gayi aur phir bhi rahi.
Ye qissa itna toota-foota hai,
Ki shabdo ki katar seedhi nahi banti,
Par seedha rasta kaha kisi ko jamta hai.
Kaash, kisi mod par tujhe na khote,
Toh ye tedhe-medhe raste bhi apne hote.

69 -kal shab

Kal shab bhi tumhe yaad kiya maine,
Jab yaad krta hu koshish krta hu,
Ek dafe baat krne ki..
Ghantiyan baj rahi thi kal bhi,
Dimaag mein baatein chal rahi thi,
Ki kya bolunga, kaise shuru krunga,
Kya baat hogi tumhara jawab kya hoga,
Par phir ghanti tham jaati hai.
Shabd hai mujhe, awaz fir tham jaati hai...
Kabhi sochta hu ki sab badal gaya,
Kabhi lagta hai cheen gaya mujhse,
Kabhi lagta hai qissa hi to tha,
Beet gaya.....
Baat ye hai ki insaani awazein,
Badi bhayanak hai,
Na dabti hain, na shant hoti hain,
Ke jaise har awaz zinda hai,
Jee rahi hai mere kaano me,
Ke jaise tu fir chu gayi, ke jaise
Tu kuch keh rahi hai kaano mein par,
Ye aawazein hai ki badafa
Sunne nahi deti.

70 - Insaan kaate

Kisi ko dhrm baate, Kisi ko karn baate,
Koi bhala usko sabse, Uska mann baate
Koi padhe haj nauha, koi hai bhajan gaate,
Koi uparwale ke naam pe insaan kaate.
Na koi desh nahi ghar sab tamasha hai,
Karz hai zindagi ye karz bhi chukana hai,
Kyu kahi kisiko uthana ya jhukana hai,
Kyu kahi kisi ko basana ya mitana hai,
Tera hai apna ya ki mera ye zamana hai,
Khoon bahane ka ye kya naya bahana hai.
Sabhi se keemti ek aam insaan hai,
Jo bhuka mar raha hai peshe se kisaan hai,
Kisi ki geeta kahi bible aur quran hai,
Dhyan se dekho hum sabhi to inaaan hai..
Wahi hai gehu wahi roti wahi khana hai,
Arth ko smjho to sabhi ka ek gana hai,
Kisi Ko loot kar ke kya tumhe kamana hai,
Duje ki jaan pe kya tera baynama hai..

Desh azad par hum soch ke ghulam hain,
Hindustani nahi hum hindu musalman hain,
Bhule hain unko k jinhone apni jaan di thi,
Humne jo baat diya ye unka hindustan hai,
Ghulam hota to smjhta iss azadi ko,
Dhyan se dekh chaaro or ki barbaadi ko,
Insaani hulia naya zaria hai batware ka,

Maut se darte hain sab pandit ho ya qazi ho..
Sab kuch wo dekhenge sabse shahenshah hain,
Chahe keh bhole chahe unko ab tu allah keh.
Jo bhi kamaya sab yahi pe reh jana hai,
Chita ya kabr tujhe dhul me mil jana hai.
Mitti ke tan ko chahe kitna hi sajale tu,
Miitti hi bete iska aakhri thikana hai..
Niyat badal jo kuch badal dikhana hai,
Chahat luta sabko saath leke chalna hai,
Aisa ban yaara jiske imaan me chhal na hai,
Aaj ki duniya hai kisi ka koi kal na hai..
Thodi mohabbat hi ye aakhri sahara hai,
Sir jhuka ke jeena kab kisiko gawara hai,
Shaan se jeena hai toh sir ucha uthana hai, Izzat kamao kahe ko paisa kamana hai.

Apne darwaze se pehle, Dekho mohalle ko
Jo hisse baate uske naam ko na halle do,
Maa baap ko izzat de usi me saari jannat hai,
Chahe fir puja kr tu Friday ko ya Sunday ko.
Chain ki saans aur sukoon ki kamai kr,
Khanjar uthana hai to bass utha burai par,
Asifa Nirbhaya ki saanso ka tu badla le,
Isse gar khauf hai chup reh aur shanti rakh.
Duniya badlne ki suni hai hunkaar sabki,
Chahe vikaas ho buri hai sarkar sabki?
Naye zamane ka ye kya naya tamasha hai,
Pahnenge mehnga par sasti khani hai roti sabzi.

VORDS: Vinci on a roadside

www.ingramcontent.com/pod-product-compliance
Lightning Source LLC
Chambersburg PA
CBHW020555030426
42337CB00013B/1105

* 9 7 8 9 3 8 8 2 7 7 3 7 2 *